MONSTER KNOWS NUMBERS

10 7 1 9 6 8 4 3 2 5

PICTURE WINDOW BOOKS
a capstone imprint

BY LORI CAPOTE   ILLUSTRATED BY CHIP WASS

I'm SILLY and SLOPPY.

My room is a mess,
full of wonderful junk.

Like what? Can YOU guess?

Something smells icky.
I love that, DON'T YOU?

Look! It's 1 sweaty basketball shoe.

3

My jump-rope snakes *HISS*.
Can you count them?

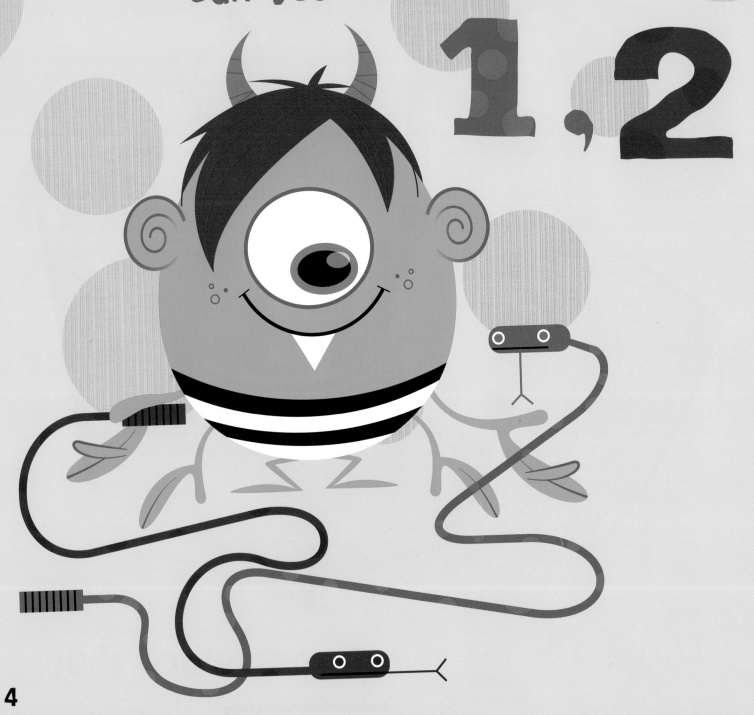

1,2

3 prickly bears
want to HUG you!

Let's blow giant bubbles!
All 4 bottles drip.

Count **5** ripped-up sails on that **HUGE** pirate ship.

6 COCKROACH cookies

make GREAT morning snacks.

7 bats hang down.
It's time to RELAX!

COUNT **8** slimy frogs as they leap out at YOU!

Watch out for 9 yo-yos all covered in GOO!

10 ducks in the tub—

Not one of them floats.

11 wind-up cows are **MAA-AHH-ING** like goats!

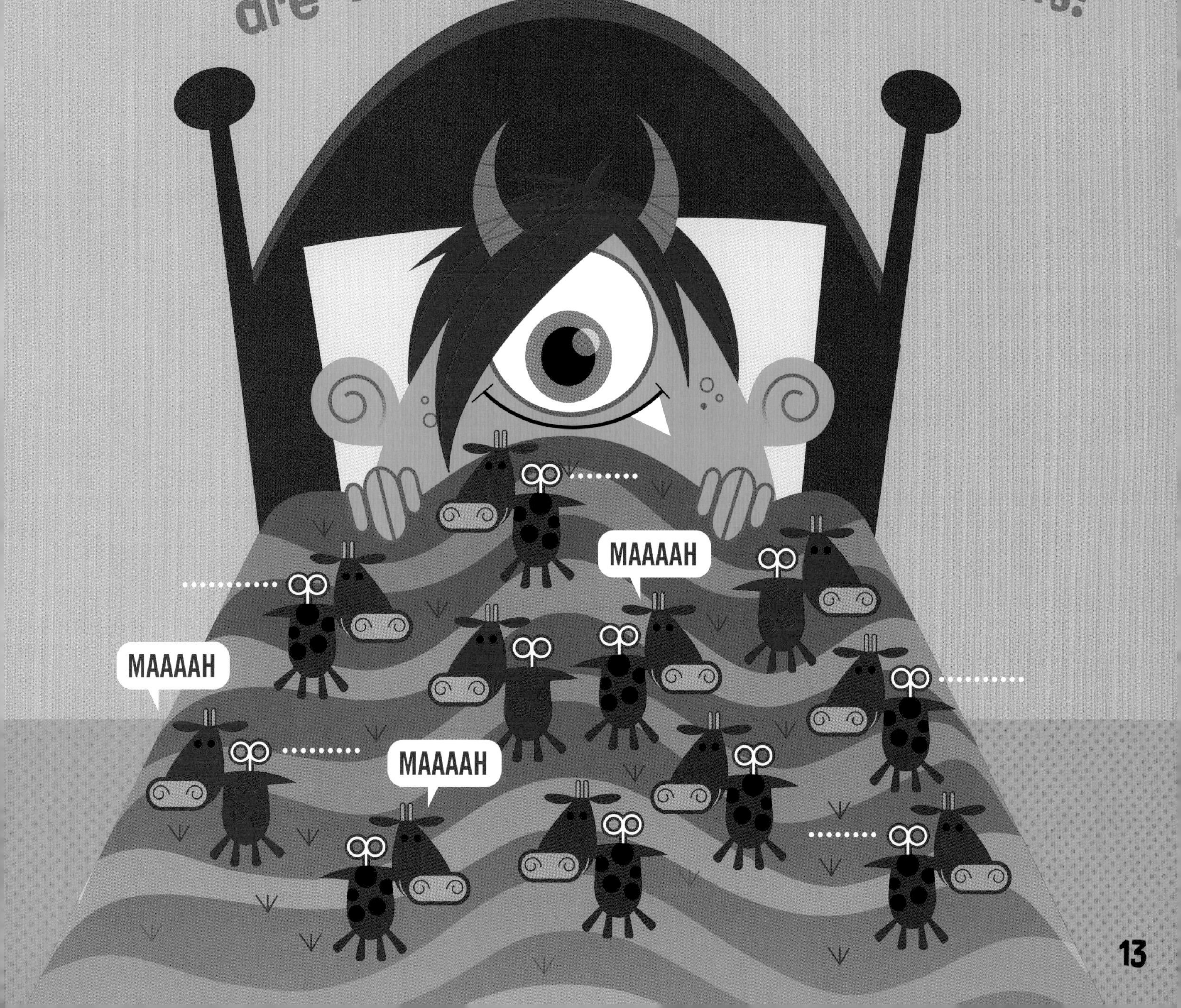

12 holey socks won't cover my TOES!

13 puzzle pieces—
but where is the **NOSE?**

 **14** worms are **SQUIRMING** in dirt.

LOOK!
15 blue eyeballs are glued to this shirt.

GLUE

17

16 dust bunnies hop into my lap.

17 spitballs

go **SPLAT** on this map!

18 moldy fries—

WOW, these taste good!

19 blocks crumble.

Bugs nibbled the wood.

Should we play with marbles?

All **20** are SQUARE!

I've counted my toys,
and I'm ready to share.

You helped me so much.
Come and play, if you dare!

Internet Sites

FactHound offers a safe, fun way to find Internet sites related to this book. All of the sites on FactHound have been researched by our staff.

Here's all you do:

Visit *www.facthound.com*

Type in this code: 9781404879461

Super-cool stuff! Check out projects, games and lots more at **www.capstonekids.com**

Look for all the books in the series:

MONSTER KNOWS MORE THAN LESS THAN
BY LORI CAPOTE ILLUSTRATED BY CHIP WASS

MONSTER KNOWS NUMBERS
BY LORI CAPOTE ILLUSTRATED BY CHIP WASS

MONSTER KNOWS PATTERNS
BY LORI CAPOTE ILLUSTRATED BY CHIP WASS

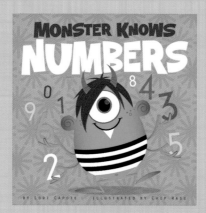

MONSTER KNOWS SHAPES
BY LORI CAPOTE ILLUSTRATED BY CHIP WASS

Thanks to our adviser for his expertise, research, and advice:
Terry Flaherty, PhD, Professor of English
Minnesota State University, Mankato

Editor: Shelly Lyons
Designer: Ashlee Suker
Art Director: Nathan Gassman
Production Specialist: Laura Manthe
The illustrations in this book were created digitally.

Picture Window Books are published by Capstone,
1710 Roe Crest Drive, North Mankato, Minnesota 56003
www.capstonepub.com

Library of Congress Cataloging-in-Publication Data
Capote, Lori, 1966-
Monster knows numbers / by Lori Capote ; illustrated by Chip Wass.
pages cm. — (Monster knows math)
ISBN 978-1-4048-7946-1 (library binding)
ISBN 978-1-4048-8038-2 (board book)
ISBN 978-1-4795-0183-0 (ebook PDF)
1. Counting—Juvenile literature. 2. Numbers, Natural—Juvenile literature. I. Wass, Chip, 1965- illustrator. II. Title.
QA113.C356 2013
513.2'11—dc23   2012029716

Artistic Effects
Shutterstock, background texture (throughout)

Printed in the United States of America in
North Mankato, Minnesota.
092012   006933CGS13